D1524335

Saints for Kids

32 Friends of Jesus

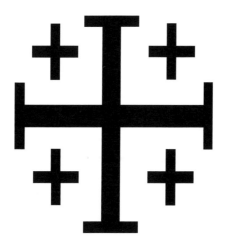

ORTHODOX STUDY GUIDE

ISBN: 9781729229194

Saints for Kids

Twenty-one out of the 32 people featured on this video are saints in the Orthodox Church. The other eleven featured are Roman Catholic, coming after the Great Schism. Several things may be noted about those persons featured in this film.

Saints are people like us who have struggled to trust God and love Him and follow His commandments. By trusting in God and showing their love for God by following His commands to love others, forgive, and put the Lord first in everything, they grew spiritually and became more holy. That is why they are called "saints," because the word "saint" means "someone who is holy" by getting closer to God.

The saints remind us that we too, as Orthodox Christians, are called by our Baptism to become saints by learning to trust God and show our love and commitment to Him by being obedient to His commandments and living an Orthodox Christian life of love and service to God and others. We become better friends of Jesus through personal prayer, attention during the liturgical prayers of the Church, fasting, doing acts of charity, and following the commands of Christ. As we struggle to become more like our Master, Christ, the Holy Spirit will help us on our spiritual journey. The saints and holy angels will also help us along the way.

Notes on Featured Orthodox Saints

The Holy Theotokos and Ever-Virgin Mary

Orthodox Christians do not usually refer to the Holy Theotokos as the "Mother of Jesus." Truly, she is His Mother, but, out of reference and as a statement of faith, they usually call her the "Theotokos" ("the one who gave birth to God"), the "Panagia" (the All-Holy), or "the Mother of God."

The Holy Theotokos is remembered at every liturgy of the Orthodox Churches. Her special feast days are September 8 (The Nativity of the Theotokos), November 21 (The Presentation of the Theotokos), December 9 (The Conception of the Theotokos), March 25 (The Annunciation to the Theotokos), August 15 (The Dormition of the Theotokos), and various feast days celebrating sundry wonderworking icons and relics of the Mother of God.

Saint Lucian of Antioch

Saint Lucian the Hieromartyr of Antioch was a very pious scholar of the Bible. He studied both the Hebrew and Greek texts of Holy Scripture and sought to elucidate the meanings of Scripture by comparing the Hebrew with the Greek. Although some of his ideas may not have been completely Orthodox, taking him for a while away from the Church, he, nevertheless, was reconciled with the Orthodox Church and is esteemed as a great scholar and martyr for Christ. His feast day is October 15.

Saint Anthony the Great

Saint Anthony the Great of Egypt is highly esteemed among Orthodox Christians. He is often called "the Father of Monasticism," although other holy men and women were led by God to dwell in the wilderness before him. Saint Athanasius the Great of Alexandria wrote a biography of Saint Anthony the Great. His feast day is January 17.

Saint Paul the Apostle

Prior to his conversion to Christ, Saint Paul the Apostle was a Jewish scholar by the name of Shaúl, or Saul, from the tribe of Benjamin. His father was a Roman citizen and therefore Paul enjoyed the rights of Roman citizenship from birth. Paul was from Tarsus in Anatolia, but studied in Palestine under Gamaliel the Elder, a grandson of the great Jewish rabbi Hillel the

Elder. The Holy Apostle Paul is commemorated together with the Holy Apostle Peter on June 29.

Saint Valentine of Rome

Saint Valentine of Rome has been honored in the Western Church from early times as a great martyr. There are also several other saints with the name Valentine. His feast day is February 14.

Saint Joseph the Betrothed

Saint Joseph of Nazareth is not called the "Husband of Mary" in the Orthodox Church. He was a widower, much older than the Holy Virgin Mary when he took her under his care. In so doing, he become engaged, or betrothed, to her, but not fully married, protecting her and her virginity. He is also called the Righteous Joseph the betrothed. His feast day is the Sunday after the Nativity of Christ, however, if there is no Sunday between December 25 and January 1, his feast is celebrated on December 26 along with King David and Saint James the Just.

The Holy Apostle and Evangelist Mark

Saint Mark the Evangelist recorded his account of the Gospel of Jesus Christ under the preaching of the Apostle Peter. He is also known as John Mark. He founded the Church of Alexandria. He is commemorated on April 25, September 27, October 30, and January 4.

Saint Ida of Killeedy

Saint Ida of Killeedy was born in A.D. 480 in Ireland. Her name means "Thirst," because of her thirst for God. She faced much opposition as she sought to adopt a monastic lifestyle. She founded a monastery for women in Kileedy, Ireland and a school for boys. One of her students was Saint Brendan. She was granted prophetic and miraculous gifts from God. A Holy Well near her grave was said to heal smallpox and other diseases. She is commemorated on January 15.

The Holy Apostle Peter

Saint Peter is not called "the first Pope" in the Orthodox Church. He is honored together with the Apostle Paul as a leader of the Church. He is called the First-Enthroned of the Apostles because it was he who first confessed Jesus as "the Christ, the Son of Living God." As such, he is the first in honor among his Apostolic equals. Contrary to the Latin accounting, in the Church,

Saint Peter does not rank in authority above the other Apostles, but is their equal in authority while being given first place in honor. He commemorated together with the Apostle Paul on June 29.

Saint Benedict of Nursia

Saint Benedict of Nursia is the founder of Western Monasticism. He did not found "the Order of Saint Benedict," since in his time the Western Church did not have different monastic orders like it does today. He did, however, write a set of monastic rules to be followed by himself and his fellow monks, basing it on the monastic writings of Saint John Cassian, who had lived among the monks of Palestine and the Egyptian desert.

Saint John Cassian, upon whose writings Saint Benedict based his monastic way of life, is venerated as a saint in the Orthodox Church, but not in the Roman Catholic Church. Saint John Cassian was Orthodox in his teachings and taught the doctrine of synergy or cooperation between Divine Grace and human will. The Orthodox doctrine of Divine/human cooperation was opposed by the extremism of Augustine's views which detract from the role of the human will in salvation. The Latin Church accepts Augustine as an expounder of correct Church doctrine and, therefore, rejects the teachings of the Holy Desert Fathers, of Saint John Cassian and of the Orthodox Church regarding the necessary cooperation between the human will and the Divine will.

Since Benedict of Nursia followed the belief and practice of the Holy Desert Fathers, he is highly-esteemed in the Orthodox Church. Saint Benedict's monastic rules are now called "The Rule of Saint Benedict." The Rule became so popular among Western monks that Saint Benedict is often called the founder of Western Christian Monasticism, even though there were monks, like Saint John Cassian, in Western Europe before him. His feast day is March 14.

The Holy Ancestors of God Joachim and Anna

Joachim and Anna, or Anne, were a childless, elderly couple. Joachim was of the tribe of Judah and a descendant of King David. Anna's father was a priest and her mother from the lineage of King David. Joachim and Anna lived in the first century B.C. After much prayer for offspring, Anna, who had been barren, became pregnant by Joachim following an angelic visitation. Anna gave birth in her old age to the Holy Theotokos and Ever-Virgin Mary. Having promised their child to God prior to her conception, Joachim and Anna ended up taking their young daughter, Mary, to live in the Temple when she was only three years old. Thus they fulfilled the vow they had made since their prayers for offspring were answered. Their feast day is September 9. The Dormition of Saint Anna is commemorated on July 25.

The Holy Apostle and Evangelist Matthew

The Holy Apostle Matthew was a man named Levi who was working as a tax collector in Capernaum when Christ called him to become one of His disciples. His name was changed to "Matthew," meaning "Gift of the Lord." After the Resurrection of Christ, Matthew wrote his Gospel in Aramaic, the spoken language of his Jewish contemporaries in Judea and Galilee. Saint Matthew left the Holy Land and traveled to Ethiopia where he preached the Gospel and was martyred for Christ. His Gospel was translated into Greek and popularized. He is commemorated on November 16 and also on the Feast of the Twelve Apostles on June 30.

The Holy Apostle and Evangelist Luke

Saint Luke was one of the Seventy Apostles sent out by Christ to preach in the Holy Land. Luke was a Greek-speaking Hellenic Jew from Syrian Antioch. He was a physician, a writer, and an artist and is responsible for the first Holy Icons of the Holy Theotokos and of the Holy Apostles Peter and Paul. He is the father of Christian iconography. He encountered the Risen Christ on the road to Emmaus. He was present in the upper room when the Holy Spirit descended at Pentecost. He wrote his Gospel in Greek after consulting with the earliest eyewitnesses of Christ, including the Holy Virgin Mary herself. He traveled with the Holy Apostle Paul from Antioch to Rome. He wrote the Acts of the Apostles also in Greek. After Saint Paul was martyred, Saint Luke preached in Italy, Egypt, Libya, Macedonia, and Greece, where he was finally martyred at age 84 in the Greek town of Thebes. He is commemorated on October 18, April 22, June 20, and January 4, the Synaxis of the Seventy Apostles.

Saints Zechariah and Elizabeth

The Righteous Zechariah, whose name is also written as "Zachariah" or "Zacharias," was a priest in the temple at Jerusalem from the lineage of Aaron. He was the Father of Saint John the Baptist, the Forerunner of Christ. Zechariah was a prophet. He was slain between the Altar of Burnt Offerings and the Porch of the Temple by King Herod's command when Herod discovered that his son had escaped the slaughter of the Innocents. The Holy Prophet and Priest Zechariah, the father of the Forerunner, is commemorated on September 5 and also on June 24, the Nativity of Saint John the Baptist.

The Righteous Elizabeth, the wife of Saint Zechariah and the mother of Saint John the Baptist, was given the gift of prophecy by which she called the Holy Theotokos "Blessed" and announced her as the Mother of the Lord. Saint Elizabeth is the niece of Saint Anna, the mother of the Theotokos. Saint Elizabeth's grandfather was a priest in the temple at Jerusalem. After John the Baptist and Christ were born, Herod tried to kill all the children two years old and under. Saint Elizabeth fled with her son John into the wilderness to escape Herod's sword, but some of Herod's soldiers followed them. God then caused a miracle to occur: a hill split open, forming a place where Saint Elizabeth and the Holy Forerunner were able to hide. Saint Elizabeth died forty days after her husband Zechariah was killed in the Temple, but Saint John the Baptist was sustained by God in the wilderness. Saint Elizabeth is commemorated the same days as Saint Zechariah, September 5 and June 24.

Saint Martin the Merciful, Bishop of Tours
Saint Martin of Tours was born to pagan parents. His father was a Roman officer. Martin served in the Roman army. He became a catechumen and decided to be baptized after receiving a vision of Christ commending him for an act of mercy he showed to a poor beggar. He became a disciple of Saint Hilary of Poitiers. Both Saint Hilary and Saint Martin preached the doctrine of the Holy Trinity against the anti-Trinitarian heresy of Arianism. He established a monastery and became a great preacher and teacher. He became bishop of Tours and lived an austere monastic life as a cave-dwelling cenobite. He is commemorated on November 11.

Saint Cecilia

Saint Cecilia took a vow of virginity, but her pagan parents forced her to marry a pagan nobleman named Valerian. Even though she was forced to marry Valerian against her will, Cecilia sang in her heart to God like the Holy Apostles Paul and Silas sang when they were imprisoned in Philippi. She warned Valerian that she was protected by an angel and promised him that if he would be baptized, he would be able to see her guardian angel. Valerian chose to be baptized and God opened his eyes to see Cecilia's guardian angel. After that, Valerian was martyred and then so was Cecilia. Her home was later converted into a church. In 1599, her body was found to be still incorrupt. Her feast day is November 22.

The Holy Apostle Andrew the First-Called

Saint Andrew was the first Apostle called by Jesus Christ. He is the brother of the Holy Apostle Peter, whom he brought with him to meet Jesus. He preached in Georgia, Byzantium, Thrace, Peloponnese, Epirus, Greece, and the area of modern Ukraine. He planted a cross on the hills of Kiev and prophesied there would be a future Christian city there. He was martyred in Patras in Peloponnese on an "X"-shaped cross. Immediately prior to his death, Uncreated Light shone from him for about a half hour as he hung on the cross until the moment when he fell asleep in Christ. His feast day is November 30. He is the patron saint of many places, including Russia, Romania, Ukraine, and Scotland.

Saint Nicholas the Wonderworker

Saint Nicholas was born to affluent parents in the city of Patara in Asia Minor. He became known for his many acts of charity and devotion and made pilgrimages to the Holy Land and to the holy sites of Egypt. He became the Archbishop of Myra in Asia Minor and suffered imprisonment under the persecutions by Emperor Diocletian. He was released from prison when Emperor Constantine legalized Christianity. Bishop Nicholas defended the worship of the Holy Trinity against the anti-Trinitarian heresy of the Arians. It is believed he attended the Council of Nicaea in A.D. 325. After his repose, he saved a group of sailors during a storm in the Aegean and became known as the patron of mariners. He became very popular as a giver of gifts and came to be called "Sinterklaas" among the Dutch—a name which developed into the modern-day "Santa Claus." His feast day is December 6.

Saint Ambrose of Milan

Ambrose was born to Christian parents in Trier, Germany. His father was a Roman official. Ambrose was educated in Rome and became a public official headquartered in Milan. He remained a catechumen through the early years of his adulthood. He became a major proponent of the Trinitarian Faith of Nicaea and argued against the Arian heresy. He was chosen to be bishop of Milan before he was even baptized. He was quickly baptized and finally ordained bishop within a matter of days. He devoted himself to the study of theology and the service of the Church in Milan. He is credited with introducing antiphonal chanting within the Church's worship. He encouraged Emperor Theodosius to repent for his massacre of Thessalonians. He was a controversial politician and an excellent administrator. He was also a great preacher of the Faith and greatly influenced the conversion of Augustine of Hippo. His feast day is December 7.

Saint Lucía the Virgin-Martyr

Saint Lucy of Syracuse, Sicily, or Saint Lucia, was the daughter of Roman nobility. After her father died, her mother, named Eutychia, found herself suffering of dysentery for several years. Lucy took her mother to pray at the tomb of the martyr-saint Agatha of Palermo. While the spent the night at the tomb in prayer, Lucy received a vision of Saint Agatha, telling her that she would suffer martyrdom. At that very moment her mother was healed. Lucy vowed virginity in devotion to Christ and gave her wealth to the poor. When she refused to marry a pagan, she was accused of being a Christian, was arrested, and forced to live in shame. But Lucy was not overcome by shame, but kept her heart pure before God. For this the pagans hated her and tried to burn her alive, but God put out the fire. Finally, she was put to death by the sword and fell asleep in Christ. Saint Lucy is remembered in the Orthodox Church on December 13. The Feast of Saint Lucia is especially celebrated in Italy and in Scandanavian countries.

The Holy Apostle Stephen the Protomartyr

Saint Stephen was a Hellenistic Jew, living in Jerusalem, who converted to Christ through the preaching of the Apostles. He was noted for his gift of teaching and preaching and his ability to perform miracles through the power of the Holy Spirit working in him. About one year after the first Pentecost of the Church, Stephen defended his faith in Christ before the Sanhedrin, the Jewish officials in Judea. Many responded to his declaration by maligning him through deceit. On account of his testimony, he was stoned to death by the Jews while Saul of Tarsus, prior to his conversion, looked on. The Most Holy Theotokos and Saint John the Theologian watched the killing of Saint Stephen from a nearby hill, praying for Stephen as he died. His feast day is December 27, but he is also commemorated on August 2 and June 15.

Notes
on
Some Featured Roman Catholics

Francis and Clare of Assisi

Of all of the uniquely Roman Catholic saints featured on this video, Saint Francis of Assisi and his contemporary female counterpart, Saint Clare are the earliest and, perhaps, the closest to the Orthodox Faith. Francis died in 1226 and, a year and a half later, was recognized as a saint in the Roman Catholic Church. The phenomena called "stigmata," exhibited in several notable Roman Catholics, such as Francis of Assisi, have only occurred twice in the recorded history of Eastern Christians and only on the margins of Orthodox Christianity: in a twentieth-century, Lebanese Orthodox female mystic who married a Roman Catholic and in a Jacobite Syrian Christian nun. Many Orthodox Christian writers from the Russian tradition argue that such people are all in a state of "prelest," or "spiritual delusion," suffering from the greatest sin, which is pride. It is a harsh judgment and one might well question the level of pride it takes to make such a judgment. Yet, perhaps, they are right in their assessment. Francis of Assisi has been scrutinized and critiqued with a fine-tooth comb by some Orthodox writers and has been deemed unworthy of being called a saint for many reasons which they are able to supply amply. Perhaps, they are right. But, then again, were such scrutiny applied to all saints, perhaps many hitherto-deemed "Orthodox" would also fall short by their exacting standards. One statement can indeed be spoken with certainty though: the tradition of **romantic** mysticism finding its nascent origins in Francis of Assisi is a digression from the spirituality of the saints of the Orthodox Church.

Thomas Aquinas

Thomas Aquinas reframed many points of the Christian Faith in Aristotelian philosophical categories. Many of his teachings were rejected by the later disciples of Saint Francis, but for a long time his teachings were even used to train Orthodox Christian seminarians. Currently, however, his more philosophical approach to matters of Faith is looked down upon by many, if not most Orthodox scholars.

There seems to be definite conflict between the thought of Aquinas and Saint Gregory

Palamas in the way they define "essence" and "energies." In some ways, Thomas Aquinas may be closer in thought to Barlaam of Calabria (St. Gregory Palamas's opponent) than to St. Gregory himself. More comparative study begs to be conducted between the teachings of Aquinas, the Franciscan monk Bonaventure, and the Hesychast Tradition of Saint Gregory Palamas.

Aquinas wrote a treatise "Against the Doctrines of the Greeks," in which he argues for Latin Catholic tradition against Greek Orthodox tradition while, at the same time, acknowledging pseudo-conflicts resulting from faulty translations between Greek and Latin. Had Aquinas had better access to Orthodox scholarly writings, he, perhaps, would not have been so critical. He was heir to a tradition already steeped in centuries of anti-Orthodox polemics.

Made in the USA
Middletown, DE
22 March 2023

27355085R00015